the chronicle of a 20 something girl

As I blew the birthday candle on my 20th birthday and made my wish. I knew that this was the decade when everything was going to change. Yet I had no clue where I was heading.

contents

change and awakening 1

love and other things 44

lost and found 90

change and awakening

"And what do you wish to be when you grow up", they asked me.

"I wish to be happy forever and always", I answered.

I felt homesick for something I couldn't put my finger on.

I accidentally found myself listening to a song I hadn't
heard since my teenage years,
and suddenly I was right back.
Not in time, but the feeling was still there.
Isn't it funny how everything, yet nothing changes at the
same time?

As I walked into my childhood home, I realized that
everything had remained the same,
yet nothing felt like before.

A small step is still a step.

On the night of my graduation,
I left the graduation party for a short while to watch the sunset.
I needed a moment for myself,
a moment to acknowledge that this beloved chapter of my life had come to an end.
Letting myself feel all the emotions.
As I stood up, I said goodbye to the old chapter and welcomed the new one.

"Have groceries always been this expensive?"
I asked my mom. "Pretty much, you just haven't had to pay for them till now",
She answered.

The city is not the same without you in it.

When did everything change? I'm looking for clues I can't seem to find.
Did it happen overnight, or did it creep up on us, slowly but surely, without us noticing?
All I know is that life is not the same it was five years ago, yet I can't remember the turning point.

I think back to a time when I was a little girl.
A little girl filled with so much hope and joy.
A little girl that believed in the goodness of the world.
A little girl that had not yet been exposed to the harsh reality.
From time to time, I wonder if it's better to be unaware than aware,
life just seems easier that way.

I had growing pains, not in my body, but my soul.

As I sat down to pay my first bill, I remember thinking, "Why didn't they teach us this in school?".

I miss my grandfather's warm hugs.

I miss looking out the car window watching the moon follow me home.

I miss waking up on Christmas morning running to the Christmas tree,
to see what Santa left for me under it

I miss being exhausted after playing on the block all day.

I miss the imagination I once had.

I wish that I could just get a day, a day to be a child again. To just one more time feel the ease that I once carried with me at all times.

Time changes everything, for better and for worse,
yet there is no stopping it. It's a never-ending ride with
bumps, loops, highs and lows, and all we can do is enjoy
it while it lasts.

No, I'm not where I thought I would be right now, and that's okay,
because the story isn't over yet, it has just begun.

Paradoxically there's no good without bad,
one is the price of the other.

"Unfortunately, we have decided to move forward with candidates"

Email after email. Rejection after rejection.

Student loans are taken to apply for the jobs that need "the new generation".

Yet they look for a "minimum of 3 year's experience", but we just graduated from college

How are we supposed to succeed in a system that is set up to fail?

Everything seems quite ambiguous, but what do I know? I'm just a 20 something girl.

When I stopped listening to others' opinions,
and instead started listening to my heart, everything
changed for the better.

For the first time in my life, I did something for myself only.
I did not need the validation nor the praise of others, because it was enough for me, and that was really all that mattered.

I try not to get sucked into the motions of life,
because one day, all of this will just be a memory.

I will no longer be twenty-three,

I will no longer live at home with my parents

I will no longer be young and free in the same way I am today.

So, try to fully embrace this moment,
because God knows I will miss this one day.

As I sat and listened to "Big girls don't cry" by Fergie,
I was thrown back to being a little girl, listening to the same exact song.
I believed that when I became a big girl, there would be no more crying.
I couldn't have been more wrong.
From time to time, life becomes disappointing, overwhelming and heartbreaking, and in those moments, the easiest thing we can do is cry.
To let all the emotions out so we can move forward.
So I guess that is what big girls do. They cry.

Sometimes I want to stomp my feet on the ground and yell out loud
"Is this some kind of joke"? Because everything is changing.
So fast that I can't seem to get a grasp of it, yet I stand still, unmovable.
They taught us everything in school, yet they forgot to tell us such an important part:
Time is a fleeting thing.

The moment we learn to let go of the things that no longer serve us, we become unstoppable.

I appreciate my alone time,
because it's then I really get to know myself.

The goal is never to stop feeling,
but rather to learn to sit with the pain,
allowing it to be there,
knowing it will pass.

I don't know,
but then again where would all the fun be if we knew everything.

Doing things out of pressure won't take you far, doing them out of pleasure will, however.

As a little girl I would rarely speak my truth,
not wanting to be anybody's burden.
As a young female I can no longer do so.
I must protect the little girl still living inside of me.

I love and hate being in my twenties.

I love having the freedom to make my own decisions,
but I hate that it's so hard making them.

I love the paycheck at the end of each month,
but I hate that I no longer have the spare time I had
before.

I love being able to travel alone and with friends,
but I hate that time seems to fly by so much faster than it
did before.

I love that I have matured, but I hate that I now see the
risks in everything.

I love that I got my bachelor's degree, but I hate that my
school years are officially over.

I have a love and hate kind of relationship with this stage
of my life.

There is so much that I love, but also so much that I
miss, and that's okay, I guess.

What isn't meant to be won't be,
and we need to have faith that it's for the better.

Sometimes I cry without really knowing the reason, but I let myself do it nonetheless, because some part of me is hurting, and denying it the hurt would just be cruel.

We do not always need to feel something.
Sometimes we just need to simply be.

On some days, I feel like I have it figured out, and on some days, I cry, lying down on the kitchen floor, not knowing what to do.
I guess that's just the way of life, and that's okay.

Be brave and face the parts of life that you need to let go of. In order for you to grow.

I still feel like 17, yet I'm 23. I thought that I would feel grown up by now, just like all the cool girls in the movies. But I feel like a child in a pair of too big shoes, trying to navigate her way in this very big world.
Will one ever feel their age, or do we simply get used to it? I'm not quite sure.

I don't know, that's all I know. And for now, that needs to be enough.

A wise woman once told me not to worry.
She told me to put every worrying thought on a cloud
and let it drift away.
Because no matter the amount of worry,
we will not be able to change the outcome of things.
So, she told me to let the thoughts drift away,
and let the outcome unfold as it pleases, and, in the
meantime, enjoy what we have in front of us, now.

We are designed to search for comfort and familiarity,
yet that is exactly what prevents us from growing.
Growth is not easy, but it is inevitable,
so instead of pushing against it,
try to move with the flow of it.
That will make things a lot easier along the way.

You're not lost, you're just twenty. These will not be the years where we feel like we have it all figured out, because we truly don't.
These are the years where we slowly figure out what we want out of this life. Piece by piece we will lay this puzzle of life and one day everything will fall into place.

It's often said that your 20s are the best years, but they fail to mention about the grief
that comes with it. The grief of losing a friend who was once thought to be forever.
The grief when realizing that our childhood and teenage years are never coming back.
And the grief that comes when we realize that we aren't where we thought we would be
by now. Our 20s are fun and games, but also scary and hard, for we have entered unknown territory.

It's hard realizing that you've outgrown something, but it's important to acknowledge what your heart is trying to tell you. Growth is never comfortable but always worth it at the end.

When anxiety comes, I know that I am doing something right. Anxiety shows up when its comfort zone is threatened. But there is no growing in the comfort zone, so, while it may be uncomfortable. I know that I have a chance to grow each time it comes for a little visit.

love & friendship

We were laying on the pavement in silence watching the starry sky. I never thought that something so simple would fill my heart to the fullest.

Me and my girls will sit for hours talking about our dreams and our goals, and when I'm with them everything seems possible. Not a dream too big or to small, to dumb or to silly, they're just about right.

Silence is also an answer.

Love should never feel painful. It should feel like falling asleep to the sound of your mother whispering a sweet lullaby.

At the age of 23, I have yet to experience falling in love.

For the longest time, I thought that there was something wrong with me.

People asking me why I haven't been in a relationship yet, made me feel like it was somehow my fault.

But I came to the conclusion that it's not me. I'm perfectly fine the way I am. I just haven't found my person yet, that's all.

They have been by my side through the highest of highs, and the lowest of lows, still the love has remained. They have shown me what true love looks like, and when I one day look for my future partner, their love will be my inspiration.

And when I one day meet you I imagine the end of "Clocks" by Coldplay playing in my head, feeling grateful for finding what I've been searching for all along, home.

We were young together. We saw each other through all the good and the bad, the happy and the sad, and then we watched each other grow into the beautiful women we are today. For that I will forever be grateful.

I looked for love, for something to fill the void,

only to realize that it was the love for myself that I was missing.

One day I'll meet someone. Until then, I'll live my life, collecting all kinds of stories, so that I one day can tell my children how cool their mom was back in the golden days.

The Recipe for Heartbreak:

4 cups of late-night conversations with your girls.

2 teaspoons of driving your car with the music blasting, screaming your heart out.

2 ¼ cups of kind and loving affirmations.

5 cups of crying (or however much you think is reasonable)

½ teaspoon of a nature walk

2 tablespoons of writing down all you feel

2 cups of reminding yourself of who you are, and that no matter what, you will overcome this as well.

I adore love.

I love seeing mothers cradling their babies, whispering sweet nothings to them.

I love seeing old married couples holding hands after decades of marriage.

I love seeing friend groups laugh until they can't breathe.

I love seeing families sitting at the diner, smiling at one another.

I love that we have been gifted the ability to feel and give such a strong emotion. An emotion that can heal almost anything.

From the moment I saw you I knew that you were going to play an important part in my life. I was drawn to you, like a moth to a flame.

And if I start loving you, there will never be a day when I don't.

We always talk about the great love one finds in a partner, but never about the great love that is found in the platonic relationships we have. The love that transforms you, the love that helps you grow, and the love that makes you believe that one day you will find it in a partner, because you have witnessed true love first hand.

I really wanted it to work out, but it takes two. The day you stopped fighting for us was the day the decision was made. So, I guess this is where we part, going our own way.

You can have all of me or nothing, there is no in between. I'm not a buffet you can feast on.

I want love that will make me feel like the most lovable person on earth. Until then, I'm good on my own, with the love I have for myself.

Acceptance is the key to any relationship.

Accepting that the people around us will change, embracing their change, making the effort to get to know them, over and over again, because they are worth it.

Accepting that as we grow up, we won't have the same time for each other as we once did before, but making the best of the time we have together.

Accepting that we all are in different stages of life, showing them that even though we may not understand this new part of their life, we still stand by their side.

No one remains the same forever, nor will life. Accepting change is vital for any relationship to stand a chance in the long run. By accepting, we show that the love for them remains the same, no matter what.

We grew up together, and then apart. We always said that such a thing could never happen to us, we were too strong for that. But life doesn't care, we change without even realizing it, and one day we stood in front of each other, best friends now strangers, wondering where it all went wrong. But it was never our fault, life just happened.

I have this vision of us sitting by the beach, watching our husbands play with our children, look at each other, smiling, because everything worked out in the end.

I sometimes wonder if I'll ever find the love I'm hoping to find. I then try to remind myself that stressing over something I cannot control is very foolish, something that may very well work out in the end, and if not, then I'll at least have the love for myself.

On my twenty-third birthday, my dear friends and I stood on the balcony of the club, singing our hearts out to "Believe" by Cher. It couldn't have been more perfect.

When I think about home, I think about laughter, I think about love, and I think about the feeling of security, and it made me realize that it's not so much the place as it is the feeling.

Settling for someone is like buying the next best bag because you didn't have the patience to save up for your dream one, there will always be regret.

As I went out this weekend, I met a boy. We stood in the smoking area for hours, talking about our failed love lives. He told me that he didn't know if he really believed in love anymore, and it made me realize that it wasn't us girls– it was our whole generation. Somewhere between "L-O-V-E" by Nat King Cole and "I Like the Way You Kiss Me" by Aretmas, we had lost our belief in love. So, the question remains: where did the love go?

I miss you as much as the night sky would miss its stars.

They did not know better, and for that, I forgive them. But I cannot surpass what was. I hope that they one day know better, saving themselves and others the pain and ache they once caused me.

Love never dies, it simply escapes, coming back as a memory every once in a while, reminding us of what once was but no longer is.

With every heartache, they sat by my side, listening to me, comforting me, saying sweet words to mend my broken heart. Each time I was ready to give up on love, I looked at the strong women standing by my side, realizing that the love that mattered had always been around.

Sitting on the balcony with towels in our hair, pouring ourselves a big glass of wine, maybe even lighting a cigarette or two if we really feel like it, deciding on which outfit to wear tonight, giggling about yesterday's mess. This is my peace of mind.

I wonder if you ever think about who I may be in the same way I think about who you may be. Two unknowing souls who are yet to meet.

McDonald's after school became Saturday nights at restaurants.

Sleepovers became vacations together.

Crying over boys became crying over life.

Seeing each other every day became seeing each other once a week.

Discussing homework became discussing work.

We grew up together, girls becoming women, with everything changing, yet remaining the same.

The best types of friendships are the ones where you can sit in complete utter silence and feel as comfortable as you would by yourself. That's love and safety.

At the age of 15, I thought that I would be in a loving relationship by the age of 20.

At the age of 23, however, I have yet to experience falling in love.

I watched all my best friends fall in love, one after another, and for years I believed that something was wrong with me. With time, however, I realized that the only thing that was wrong was my own perception. There is no right age to fall in love for the first time, to find a partner, or to get married, that will come when the time is right. Things rarely turn out the way we expect them to, and maybe that's for the greater good.

My dear family and friends have taught me that love can be found in the smallest of gestures.

A short phone call to see how your day was.

Sending videos on TikTok that we relate to.

The hug you get after not seeing them for weeks.

Buying you macaroons when you feel down.

Crying with you because they know that you are going through a tough time.

Saying that the dress you're trying out fits like a glove.

There is no need for grand gestures when it comes to real love. Because the love that is collected through the everyday mundane things will keep your heart full at all times.

Yes, dates are fun. What's even more fun however, is meeting the girls for Sunday brunch. Spilling all the tea on the frogs and the princes.

Searching for love where it once broke you is like searching for water in the desert. It will never be found, it's not the right climate.

I couldn't tell you that I loved you to the moon and back, it seemed too close. So, I told you that I loved you to the end of the universe and back, that way you would know that my love for you is never ending.

I watched you grow as a mother, and you watched me grow into a woman.

You taught me all the wisdom one could be taught in life, and I taught you about TikTok.

Looking in the mirror, I see a bit more of you in myself with everyday passing, something that warms my heart. Because I will always carry a part of you.

You have loved me through all my phases, teaching me what motherhood is, and I hope to one day be half the mother you are.

Our friendship changed with time.

Just like everybody said it would

But it changed in the most beautiful way possible.

Our bond grew stronger.

The silence became comforting.

The weekly phone calls came to be daily ones.

Honesty was no longer scary.

The fear of judgment faded away

And you became a necessity I could not live without.

So yes, our friendship did change. But change isn't always bad.

I will stay in a loving relationship with myself until I can find a partnership that will add to the love, rather than subtract from it.

You taught me that actions always speak louder than words.

You held my hand when I was scared.

You sat by my side when I felt like my life was crumbling down, telling me that everything would be alright.

You showed me the importance of keeping my standard high.

And most important of all, you have taught me how important it is for me to one day choose the right father for my future children. Because I want them to feel just as safe and loved as I am.

We cried as we parted that day, unsure of what the future held. Scared that the distance would put a distance on our friendship. But we made it work.

Phone calls during our lunch breaks, debriefing the latest gossip.

Sending screenshots of the latest hinge date, debating whether there should be a second one.

Facetiming from the fitting room, always giving our honest opinion

A few weekends spent together, compensating for the time apart, always having the best time.

A solid foundation cannot be broken easily, and the same goes with friendship. Where there is love, there is a way.

Sure, boys are fun, but at the end of the day, it's the late-night conversations, the wine dates, and the crying sessions with my girls that bring light to my life.

lost and found

What is lost can always be found, you just have to look for it.

Day by day, step by day, you are getting closer to what you have been dreaming of for so long. Patience, darling, patience, you are getting there.

I always tried to fit in, to mold myself into something I was not. Until I realized that I was never supposed to fit in, I was meant to be me. So that's what I'm offering, myself. Take it or leave it.

I started to appreciate the small things in life.

Seeing my mother and father sitting on the couch watching TV, feeling thankful for having such a loving family.

Waking up early in the morning seeing the sun come in through the blinders, being thankful for another day.

Hearing birds sing, feeling thankful for the ability to experience all the beautiful things life has to offer.

I started to appreciate the things that I always thought were a given, when in reality all these things are a blessing to be thankful for each day.

Be kind, my mother told me; that's the only thing that will matter in the end; the kindness you showed towards yourself and others.

We look at other people feeling envy of what they have, because we are lacking it, forgetting that they too are fighting their own battle. The grass isn't greener on the other side.

I love going out on the weekends, but I also appreciate my weekends spent at home.

I absolutely adore treating myself to a nice bag every once in a while, but going thrifting is just as fun.

I enjoy traveling to big cities, but visiting my family in the countryside fills my heart just as much.

I love hearing juicy gossip from my friends, but I also love to have deep, meaningful conversations with them.

We do not need to categorize ourselves; it doesn't need to be either or, we can be both. The most important thing is that we stay true to ourselves, doing what we love.

And there she goes, achieving everything she has ever dreamed of, proving herself right, and everybody else wrong.

I became my own best friend.

Listening to my racing mind, trying to calm it down.

Comforting my aching heart by turning on a nostalgic chick flick.

Making chicken noodle soup, to cheer myself up.

Talking kindly and encouraging to myself, each time a doubting thought showed up.

Love begins from within.

When someone asks me what inner peace is to me, I imagine myself lying in a field of flowers on a warm summer's day. The birds are singing, and the wind is soft. There isn't a concern in the world, and I smile, because this is my inner peace.

Beauty is more than appearance.

It's smiling at strangers.

Loving yourself endlessly.

Dancing in the kitchen in your pajamas.

A heartfelt laugh shared with a loved one.

Beauty will radiate from you when you are aligned with who you really are.

When I allowed myself the time to do what I loved doing. Suddenly life wasn't so dull anymore.

When I started to take care of myself and give myself the love I longed for from others for so long, I realized just how beautiful life could be. Being able to be enough by myself.

And through it all your softness remained.

Softness is strength, don't let anybody tell you otherwise.

Repeat after me,

I am beautiful,

I am strong,

And I am kind.

Repeat and repeat until every cell in your body starts believing in the truth.

For now, it's only me and that's okay. I enjoy my lonely Tuesdays with myself and my book, my Saturday wine dates with the girls, and my Sunday dates with the city. It's all about me, and for now that's more than enough.

If you feel the need to impress your surroundings, perhaps you are in the wrong one, because in the right one you should feel enough no matter what.

Take a leap of faith instead of spending a lifetime wondering what if. Wondering what could have been will hurt far more than failing ever will.

The beauty of the soul will always outshine the exterior beauty.

The compliments you receive won't truly resonate until you start believing in them. It starts with you.

They told her to settle, to lower her standards, to stop being so picky. But she knew her worth, and knew that when the time was right, she would get the best there was.

I hope that I one day have laugh lines, showing that my life was a happy one.

I hope that I one day have wrinkles, proving that I expressed all of my emotions.

I hope that I one day have sunspots on my skin, showcasing all the time the sun kissed me.

I hope that I one day have stretch marks, proving how amazing my body is.

And I hope that I one day age gracefully, embracing all the amazing changes my body has undergone throughout the years, my body being a testimony to the beautiful life I lived.

All roses are beautiful, yet none of them are identical. Just like us.

Always listen to your heart, that's where the truth hides.

The happiness you are looking for can always be found within yourself. Just start listening to what your soul craves.

We are like art, everyone will perceive us differently, leaving a comment on what they see, yet only the artist knows the real meaning behind the creation they made.

There is nothing to be ashamed of. You are one of a kind. Stay true to yourself and let the opinions of others move through one ear and out the other. The only one who needs to understand is you.

Getting to know who you are will be among the most powerful things you learn, because when you do, the words of others simply lose their power, being what they are, words.

We will love some chapters more and some less, but it wouldn't be a good book without its ups and downs. Let the book take its course; the words are already written.

Your soul always knows what's right. There will be no way of missing it. You'll be pulled towards it like a moth to a flame.

I appreciate my single years, because there will come a day when I'll sit in the kitchen, watching my husband and children running around, thinking back to a time when it was only me, missing it from time to time. So, I'll enjoy this time while it lasts, because once it's gone, there's no coming back to it.

I like a lot of things.

I like rolling down the car window on a warm summer day, letting the wind hit my face.

I like walking barefoot on the grass.

I like sunsets and sunrises.

I like strawberries with cream.

I like reading good books.

I like laughing so much that my stomach hurts.

I like a lot of things, but these may very well be my favorites.

They told me that I was too sensitive, too kind, too soft, making me believe that my best traits were my worst.

When you think about it. It wouldn't make sense if we had it all figured out in our 20s. Our 20s are for all the trial and errors so that we one day figure out what we truly want.

So yes, I was disappointed, but instead of blaming myself for not being enough as I always did. I came to the conclusion that I was perfectly enough. I had just relied on the wrong people.

Be someone little you needed.

As I floated in the sea, looking around at the beautiful view, I felt the waves carry my body and realized that this must be what peace feels like.

I try to not get sucked into the motions of life, because one day all of this will be just a memory.

I will no longer be twenty-three.

I will no longer live at home with my parents.

I will no longer be young and free in the same way I am today.

So, I try to fully live in every moment, because God knows I will miss this one day.

When in doubt, wait it out. There is no need to rush an answer that will come to you when the time is right.

Maybe it wasn't meant for you. Not because you didn't deserve it, but perhaps because something bigger and better is waiting around the corner. Not all blessings glimmer at first sight.

You are not hard to love, and if anybody has made you feel different, I'm sorry. You deserve all the love one can get, the type of love that will make you feel like the most lovable person on this earth, because you truly are.

I want to travel the world, but I would also really like to find a city to settle down in.

I can't wait till the day I find my soulmate, yet I love being single.

I'm drawn to the easygoing pace of the countryside, but I also thrive in the fast-paced city that never sleeps.

I would love to be a stay-at-home mom, but I can't imagine a life without a career.

I'm not really sure of who I am just yet, and that's okay. I'll figure it out in time. Until then, I will keep exploring this little life.

I am still the same girl that I was when I was 10, when I was 16 and when I was 20.

I still prefer salty treats over sweet ones.

I still sing my heart out when I'm home alone.

I still cry when I see abandoned animals, children or elderly people struggling.

I still cuddle up with my mom when I'm sad or need comfort.

And I still find music to be the best therapy there is.

These are the parts of me that I have carried with me since the beginning of time, the parts of me that truly mirror who I am. Some parts have changed, that's just life, but the most important ones are here to stay, and that brings me great comfort.

Be yourself in a world full of others.

I'm learning to ask for help when I need it.

I'm learning to stay with all the uncomfortable feelings.

I'm learning to say no.

I'm learning to feel safe again.

I think that I'm healing.

At the age of 7, I wanted to be a princess.

At the age of 16, I wanted to become a lawyer.

At the age of 20, I thought that a career in marketing would be right for me.

Now, at the age of 23, I dream of one day being an author.

We can't expect our dreams to remain the same forever, but we do need to follow them when they call us, no matter how big of a detour it may be. We owe ourselves that.

I love my Norah Jones kinds of mornings.

Waking up early to the sunlight gleaming through my window.

Making myself a cup of coffee and drinking it on the balcony, while reading my book.

I've learned that joy is often found in the smallest of moments, the moments when we get to truly be ourselves.

A rose cannot grow in the desert. But the rose is not at fault for that, it is simply in the wrong environment. We cannot expect to grow where there is no water for our soul.

We achieve our goals without noticing.

In hindsight, I now see that a great number of things I once dreamed about are now reality.

We forget to give ourselves credit for the work we do and miss noticing the beautiful life we have created for ourselves, by ourselves.

Give yourself a pat on the shoulder, you've done great.

If you're standing at a crossroad, not knowing where to go, pause and choose the path that draws you. If it turns out to be the wrong one, you can always return and try another one. It is not the end of the World.

Made in the USA
Monee, IL
23 November 2024